T0067485

The Real Me

No Apologies, No People Pleasing, No Excuses for Who and What You Are!

LAURA-JANE COTE

BALBOA.
PRESS

A DIVISION OF HAY HOUSE

Copyright © 2017 Laura-Jane Cote.

All rights reserved. No part of this book may be used or reproduced by
any means, graphic, electronic, or mechanical, including photocopying,
recording, taping or by any information storage retrieval system
without the written permission of the author except in the case
of brief quotations embodied in critical articles and reviews.

Balboa Press books may be ordered through booksellers or by contacting:

Balboa Press
A Division of Hay House
1663 Liberty Drive
Bloomington, IN 47403
www.balboapress.com
1 (877) 407-4847

Because of the dynamic nature of the Internet, any web addresses or
links contained in this book may have changed since publication and
may no longer be valid. The views expressed in this work are solely those
of the author and do not necessarily reflect the views of the publisher,
and the publisher hereby disclaims any responsibility for them.

The author of this book does not dispense medical advice or prescribe the use
of any technique as a form of treatment for physical, emotional, or medical
problems without the advice of a physician, either directly or indirectly. The
intent of the author is only to offer information of a general nature to help
you in your quest for emotional and spiritual well-being. In the event you use
any of the information in this book for yourself, which is your constitutional
right, the author and the publisher assume no responsibility for your actions.

Any people depicted in stock imagery provided by Thinkstock are
models, and such images are being used for illustrative purposes only.
Certain stock imagery © Thinkstock.

Print information available on the last page.

ISBN: 978-1-5043-7284-8 (sc)
ISBN: 978-1-5043-7285-5 (e)

Balboa Press rev. date: 01/28/2017

Contents

The Real Me

Let the real you shine—no apologies, no people pleasing, no excuses for who and what you are.

Inspirational stories and exercises to live authentically. This is a guide to help you access your inner wisdom through personal spiritual tutorials Enjoy your process!

Written by:
Laura-Jane Coté

The writing of this book has been a wondrous learning experience. I am grateful to all those teachers, mentors and supporters both in the physical and non-physical world that helped bring it from concept to form.

The Real Me

Let the real you shine—no apologies, no people pleasing, no excuses for who and what you are.

As far back as I can remember, I thought it was paramount to be liked in order to be loved. If I wasn't liked, my life would be miserable. People pleasing was the way to ensure my place with my parents and extended family, school, church, community, and society. Every morsel of love was linked to the approval from all those around me. Others determined my worth by how well I satisfied their desires and needs. I believed this to be an absolute truth and never doubted this was the way I was meant to live.

As I began my spiritual awakening, things shifted. The more I communicated with Spirit, the more restless I became. Who was the authentic *me*? What did *I* truly want in life? What does it mean to be a *divine human*? I had spent my life putting everyone else's needs ahead of my own, so these were big, scary questions propelling me to reframe how I viewed and took care of myself. It meant accepting that I—and I alone—am responsible for shaping my life. Yet here is the dichotomy: I am not alone because Spirit is there to support and guide me. Learning to love myself first in order to truly love others felt foreign and beyond my capacity.

The journey has been interesting, to say the least. Busy with classes, meditation groups, and studying as a medium and energy healer, I had so much to learn. Those "ah-ha" moments were always fantastic, whereas the "ah crap" moments presented opportunities for growth. I admit a definite preference for the "ah-ha" moments but recognize the real value of the learning occasions as well.

Early on, I started keeping a journal. Some days all that made it into the journal were the angel cards I drew that day or a simple thank you to Spirit for helping me get through the day. Increasingly, I discovered I was actually writing new things—stories, ideas, poems. Over time, I came to refer to them as my Spirit tutorials. A tutor is someone who offers individualized lessons to help you gain insight into a topic.

This book is a compilation of these Spirit tutorials, with guiding questions to help you connect with and complete your personal Spirit tutorial. Not every tutorial or poem will resonate with you. That is fine; take only what speaks to you, and leave the rest. I certainly won't be offended or hurt. After all, the focus of this part of my journey is on *giving up the need for others' approval and embracing everything from a detached but loving perspective.*

As you do your work, remember you seek a divine or higher perspective of love as you create and re-create the real you. It is also from this perspective that you understand how much you are truly loved and supported on your journeys, even during the "ah crap" moments.

Remember to be gentle with yourself.
With much love, tenderness, and gratitude,

L-J

Answering the Call

WHATEVER POSSESSED ME to quit my old life and start anew? Others told me that I was courageous to walk away and head off alone. All I felt was a profound call to renew myself, let go of anything that didn't feel authentic.

A deep and restless need for change persisted, but I pushed it away and focused on the happy, contented moments I still felt—peaceful occasions spent in the yard watching the birds flitter about, listening to the bees as they gathered pollen. I had a private healing practice that was slowly growing, an expanding circle of friends, and, of course, my journaling. Above all, I spent hours in the swimming pool, for it became a place of meditation. I loved the cool water and the rhythmic movement as I swam in this weightless, sweet-smelling oasis. I floated in an almost trancelike state while watching the hummingbirds feed on the honeysuckle bushes and breathing in the scents from the flowers and lavender growing at the edge of the pool. These were contented moments, but they were not enough. I knew that soon my pool would freeze over and the hummingbirds would be replaced by the hearty chickadees and yellow finches. Winter would once more force my garden into a deep slumber. I realized that for the first time this thought truly repelled me. Every fiber of my being screamed, "No winter; it is not time to hibernate." I wanted to continue to feel the sun on my skin and experience the freedom of weightlessness in the water. I wanted to bask in a sunshine that brought me warmth, not just the glistening of frozen water crystals. My spirit rebelled at the thought of having to add layers of clothes to venture outside. I wanted to shed layers, not add to them! I wanted to continue to grow rather than go down for a long winter nap.

I felt the tropics calling me on so many levels—physical, emotional, and spiritual. Spirit heard my call and offered me the opportunity to seek my freedom. I bless and thank the Angels and Guardians who helped me understand these whisperings of my heart. The whisperings became directions that led me to a home of perpetual summer; of free, wriggling toes; and of lightness for two years in Hawaii. It was there that I shed the layers, and this book was born.

Your Own Spiritual Tutorial

- What is your spirit calling you to do now to enhance living authentically? (e.g., people, thoughts, or things to shed, release, or add to your life)

- How can you be mindful of this call? (e.g., awareness of current situations that don't support your authentic self)

- Where is your authentic self leading you? (e.g., study, travel, new relationship, starting your own business)

Releasing the Need for Approval

Pₑₒₚₗₑ ʜₐᵥₑ ₛₚₑₙₜ lifetimes seeking others' approval and conforming to others' expectations in order to be loved. Why? What is the source of this cycle? I had constructed my need for approval on a fear of losing love through disapproval. The message was clear: it was time to face this reverberating fear if I were to find my authentic self. I knew that surrendering to this fear would result in stress, anxiety, and depression.

Falling in love with myself had to be my starting point, not some narcissistic activity but a genuine belief in my own worthiness as a divine human. I had to offer myself the same kindness and compassion I so easily give to others. It was about accepting and loving all the little quirks and idiosyncrasies that make me unique. To begin, I compiled a list of a few of my quirks to learn to accept and be grateful for them: knowing I say yes when I mean no, recognizing that my compulsion for organization and neatness stems from a need to control my environment, having an aversion to any type of loud noises because they remind me of fights in the family and make me feel small, disliking socks and shoes (I don't know why), and having an eclectic taste in music that few people but me appreciate. Of course, I didn't forget the good quirks: my persistence and sense of optimism, a genuine sense of caring and compassion for others, a sense of humour (sometimes a bit dark), and my ever-strengthening connection to my inner divine.

Every day, I spent time seeing myself through the eyes of the divine. I knew that my worthiness to receive love and compassion was never questioned. I knew that Spirit would never desert me for some act of humanism that was less than perfect. I knew that, as uncomfortable as it felt, I had to see my own value and project this into the world. Every day, I still remind myself to love me as much as I love others, to respect me as I respect others, and to accept my own imperfections without judgment as I accept other people without judgment. Loving myself unconditionally has opened the door for me to love others in the same way. I am grateful for you and me. Know that *being divine is truly sublime*!

Your Own Spiritual Tutorial

- What quirks do you have? *Remember, all these quirks are part of the same divine parcel of our own creation.*

- How do you judge these quirks? (e.g., good, bad, they are how I stand out in a crowd)

- What can you do to affirm your worthiness, bless these quirks, and release self-judgment? (e.g., write affirmations that support loving yourself and all your wonderful quirks)

The Divine Mirror

Mirror, mirror, on the wall,
Do I see my true self at all?
The reflection I see is always ripe with flaws,
Yet you tell me that you are in total awe.
What do you see when you gaze upon me?
And how do I learn to see what you see?

The years on this earth have taught me too well
To focus completely on the times that I fell.
There is within me such resistance
To believe in myself as a divine existence.

Looking deep in my heart, I see something buried,
A small seed of self-love that my faith has carried.
So, with your assistance and through my persistence,
I can feel the stirrings of a small inner light,
A light that helps me see with heavenly sight,

A sight that is not based on others' views,
A sight that is centered on my own truths.
Now as I gaze upon my requested reflection,
The truth I see is my own divine perfection.

I give thanks to all my spiritual tutors for this insight.

Your Own Spiritual Tutorial

- What does your divine mirror reflect back to you?

- Is there anything stopping you from clearly seeing your divine reflection?

- How will you succeed in overcoming these challenges?

Laying Down My Burden Basket

W<small>E ALL CARRY</small> a burden basket in the physical world of time and space. Somewhere in this world of form, I wandered off and wove my burden basket from perceptions of failure and success. It consisted of intricately intertwined dramas and intense emotions, such as pride, fear, lust, hate, and sorrow. With every strand, I became reliant on the drama that made me "feel alive" in this world of form. I enjoyed the energy rush with each new crisis. Yet the emptiness that followed each made me crave another one to feel alive again. I had been carrying this ever-growing burden basket for years, insisting it remain strapped to my back. I self-righteously refused every opportunity to put it down. After all, my handwoven basket was my badge of honor showing everyone all the dramas and struggles I had endured and how valiantly I had succeeded in coping with them. Blessed with my tutorial on wisdom, I saw through Spirit's eyes that life is not meant to be a burden; rather, what was a burden was my *human* perspective of self-worth. It was time to lay down my basket, for it was a transient creation that could never bring true happiness or a sustained feeling of purpose. As I lay it down, I took Spirit's hand and knew that I had arrived at a place without high drama, prolonged struggle, or loneliness. This is an internal place where no one creates burden baskets. It is a place of unconditional love and unity with my divine self.

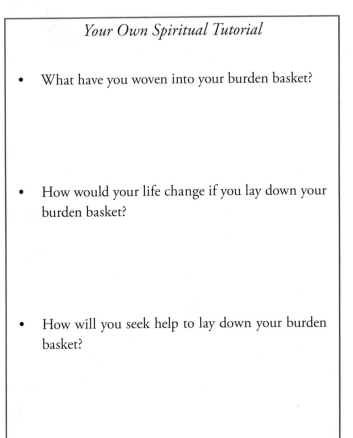

Your Own Spiritual Tutorial

- What have you woven into your burden basket?

- How would your life change if you lay down your burden basket?

- How will you seek help to lay down your burden basket?

Signposts

My SPIRITUAL STUDIES included a lot about who I was from a spiritual perspective and being my authentic self. The readings indicated that everyone's authentic state was simply *Being*. What did that mean? What should it feel like? Accepted authorities described *Being* as attending to the "here and now." Words such as *bliss*, *peace*, *love*, and *joy* describe the emotions of living authentically. Lovely, sign me up now! In the meantime, what was I to do with my feelings of anger, despair, loneliness, or hopelessness? Why was I feeling these even when staying in the present? Spirit seemed to be messing with my efforts to live as my authentic self.

Spirit, never stumped for an answer, told me that those uncomfortable emotions are barometers of my progress toward living consciously in the physical realm. Every unpleasant feeling presented me with an opportunity to find creative solutions for the challenge that created this discomfort. As creativity comes from divine inspiration, seeking creative solutions meant I was engaged in a divine activity. In fact, I was learning how to navigate divinely in this world of form to express my authentic self. One lesson came in the form of ending a long-lasting friendship I thought was based a shared spiritual connection. I felt let down, hurt, and betrayed. How could these feelings help me? The higher perspective was required. This divine view revealed that relationships, like everything, changed and evolved as I changed and evolved. Rather than painting it with judgments of unfairness or hurt, I saw it as another signpost to learn and practice divine detachment. It is a detachment from my old concepts that friendships must last forever, that issues are to be resolved together, and, most importantly, that I was responsible for another's feelings. I released my judgment and expectations about this relationship and appreciated that it had served our mutual needs and was now over. I felt gratitude for the relationship and its role in my life. I blessed the experience and released it in a loving manner. I moved from the signposts of hurt and disappointment to a place of peace and thankfulness. I recognize that the unpleasant emotions are gifts from Spirit intended to promote my growth as an authentic and divine human in this time and space.

Your Own Spiritual Tutorial

- What signposts are you dealing with in your spiritual growth and evolution? (e.g., emotions or circumstances that make you uncomfortable or you would like to change)

- What are the underlying thoughts and judgments that you are making about these signposts? (e.g., My partner should know better than to say or do that; Why aren't they grateful for my help?)

- How can you creatively reframe these to view the situation(s) from a divine perspective and detach from expectations linked to those judgments? (e.g., I am responsible for my own feelings; If I want something, I will ask for it directly and clearly)

Walking My Perfect Path

ALL I NEED to do is put one foot in front of the other to follow my perfect path. This is the perfect path of my heart that leads me to a union with my divine self. My heart recognizes every stream, every pebble, every root, and every tree on this path that we co-created. Travel along this path teaches me how to bring forward my divine essence into the world of form. My heart's path shows me how to love myself and trust my intuition. I discover that expressions of joy, love, and laughter are integral to my authentic state of being. The journey includes opportunities to ramble and explore new ideas, as well as time to rest, reflect, and meditate. All these opportunities deepen my connection with my inner divine tutor. This tutor wisely told me, *"We are all free to enjoy the heart's path and journey any way we wish."* Know that we can laugh, love, curse, sweat, slide, run, walk, and crawl, for there is no one way to travel our unique perfect path. I learn to accept that I walk the right path for me—a path infused with light and love, as well as challenges and solutions.

Your Own Spiritual Tutorial

- What does your perfect path hold for you in terms of challenges? (e.g., relationship off the rails, financial struggle, can't get a good job)

- How do you choose to travel it and engage in creative solutions? (e.g., meditate and seek inspiration from a higher source, look to books and stories of others who have faced similar challenges)

- What other ways might you travel to co-create your path with Spirit? (e.g., reframe and look at the challenge differently, seek someone to assist you)

The Pity Party

I know I am whole, complete and perfect in this very moment. Faith is this unshakable knowing that this is the true reality. Whatever I say or do is from my highest source – my God-Self that only knows, creates and supports wholeness and perfection for all life.

Even as my faith grows, I still have moments of victimhood celebrated with pity parties sporting sad decorations, dried up cake and lukewarm coffee. Mercifully these parties are diminishing and in their place there is light, peace, and gratitude. Gratitude for every lesson learned, every supporting hand, every person, every book and every vision that guides me on the path of the real me.

Living authentically requires releasing ego's perspective of life. Ego says *"be realistic what you seek is not humanly possible"* – pity party time! Pity parties see only the cloudy skies. It requires effort to raise my sight beyond these challenges and see the truth beyond my temporarily clouded vision.

To rebalance my perspective I count my blessings; I am blessed with abundance, I am blessed with health; I am blessed with love; I am blessed with my connection to spirit; I am blessed as healer; I am blessed, I am blessed.

Blessings and gratitude illuminate my higher perspective where pity parties are not held, a perspective that helps me understand that things don't have to be "humanly" possible. I can choose to trust the divinely human me that is supported and connected with the limitless blue sky and my clear vision.

Your Own Spiritual Tutorial

- When are you most likely to throw yourself a pity party? (E.g. you are feeling victimized by someone or something)

- What blessings can you identify that will help you leave these pity parties?

- What can you do on a regular basis to reduce and eventually eliminate personal pity parties? (E.g. gratitude journal, meditation, seek help from someone you trust).

Duality—A Truly Human Condition

―――――――――――――❧❧❧――――――――――――――

My LIFE HAS always been a duality between the spiritual and physical realms. The concept of duality was entrenched from birth, and I grew up with teachings such as "there are two sides to every coin" and "every story had two sides." As long as I am in physical form, I live simultaneously as a physical and spiritual being.

Awareness was my key to understanding this span between realms. The awareness of my divine perspective became a source of inner strength that helped me learn to love my physical reality. This did not happen spontaneously. In fact, in the beginning, I felt as if I were standing in the middle of a shaky suspension bridge that spanned a vast, dark gully between my spiritual and physical selves. The bridge was especially wobbly when I believed that I could live in only one reality and deemed the other as "unreal." I believed that my truth was to live within the spiritual realm, so I dismissed the physical realm as unreal. That created an endless tug-of-war that almost tore my whole being apart. My tutor patiently explained that *real* and *unreal* were judgments that I had created in my mind; there is no duality. Actually, my divine purpose is to experience all that the physical realm has to offer and express myself through it. I responded by saying if that were the case, why was I perpetually experiencing financial inadequacy and expressing that as a hand-to-mouth existence? I didn't see how that was expressing myself with any level of spiritual success! All the trust and prayer didn't do much to change my physical condition. The bridge gave a good "ah-ha" quiver, and I grabbed the rope to hang on. I remembered a previous tutorial that as a divine human I created my "reality." I had learned that my thoughts resulted in divine creation, and this creation was expressed and led to an outcome. Slowly, the light began to shine. I had created an ambivalence about my finances based on a deep personal judgment that money was the "root of all evil" and tainted. This was expressed by moments of financial stability followed by purging this evil from my life through bankruptcy. To stop the bridge from quivering, I had to rid myself of this deeply held judgment and see money for what it is: a simple exchange of energy. Money is not evil, and accepting it didn't corrupt my spiritual self. From this perspective, I created the thought that as a spiritual being it was OK to express myself through consistent healthy finances. There isn't a duality between spiritual and financial viability; rather, it was something I had created and expressed.

Today, I am aware that any duality I feel is my own creation that has been expressed in the physical realm. I also know that any sense of duality can exist only as long as I continue to create it.

Your Own Spiritual Tutorial

• What are the areas of conflict you experience between your spiritual and physical realms? (e.g., look at areas you feel torn between what you would like to do and what you actually do)

• What thoughts and/or judgments are contributing to this duality? (e.g., what are you saying to yourself that perpetuates the divide?)

• What new thoughts will overcome this duality? How will you support these new thought? (e.g., let go of judgments, create positive affirmations, accept responsibility for your thoughts and actions)

Dance of Life

I CO-CREATED MY DANCE of life with the universal divine; together, we crafted movement and choreographed each step. It is a dance of limitless joy, effortlessly synchronized with the rhythm of my heart.

Living in the world of form brought criticism by others. My choreography was different from the prescribed rules, and my rhythm diverged from the standards of the dance of life in this time and space.

I accepted these authorities of the dance of life in the world of form and felt that I was mistaken. I released my original dance and memorized the conventional steps that followed the rules. My new dance felt uncomfortable, mechanical, and difficult to learn. My heart no longer felt an easy rhythm with dance. While everyone said it was lovely, it no longer filled me with the joy and happiness I had once felt.

I asked the proclaimed authorities how to feel the joy and happiness of the dance of life. They told me the dance of life is hard and only those who are most gifted will master this dance. Furthermore, mastery of the dance of life is gained through great sacrifice and suffering. I must earn the right to perform the dance of life expertly but don't expect much, as only a gifted few are worthy to achieve this.

Saddened and disappointed, I questioned my worthiness to even try to perform the dance of life. Then, I had a dream where I performed my dance of life with perfection. The music was magical, and my soul felt free again. I knew in my heart that everyone has the gift of freedom to perform his or her own unique dance.

My dream gave me the courage to return to the dance of life that I had co-created with my divine. I began performing my dance of life with small steps that grew larger every day. My confidence grew as I leaned to trust in my worthiness. Once again, my dance became the limitless creation that did not conform to others' rules of time and space. My dance of life moved to the beat of my heart and the rhythm of my soul. It is infused with trust in myself and faith in Spirit's continuous love and support.

Love your dance of life, and move freely and confidently, knowing it is perfection.

Your Own Spiritual Tutorial

- What are the areas of your dance of life that bring you unlimited joy and happiness?

- How is your dance of life controlled by allowing others to tell you how to perform it?

- What can you do to take control and responsibility for your unique dance of life?

Compassionate Communication

I THOUGHT THAT "FAILURE to communicate" meant engaging in arguments and stubbornly insisting that the other person didn't understand me. Or worse, I became enmeshed in the other's story and needed to fix him or her. My communications with Mum travelled this route, leaving me with a sense of being responsible to *create a successful outcome,* always. Mum defined *successful* as getting what she wanted and my acceptance of her point of view. This pattern of communication didn't serve either of us, and I discovered that I followed this same pattern with others in my life. With Spirit's guidance, I learned a process I called "compassionate communication," which means being aware of the *entire* communication process and listening and responding with love and an open mind. In other words, it is communicating with empathy and without judgment. Empathy focuses on the feelings part of the message—that is, both the other person's and mine. Listening without judgment keeps me present rather than jumping to conclusions or preparing my response. In Mum's case, I became more attuned to her feelings of pain, anger, sorrow, joy, or whatever she was expressing. The bigger challenge was not reacting to those strong emotions by making judgments based on experiences or patterns. When I responded with an open mind, I became less attached to the outcome and more engaged in the feelings and ideas she was expressing. As a result, I became less reactive to her *story* and released my need to *control her feelings and the outcome of the communication.*

I learned that with practice, compassionate communication requires truly caring enough to listen from a higher perspective and respect that everyone is responsible for his or her own journey. This type of communication enabled me to access my own wisdom and gave others the space to do the same. I realize now I am not responsible for another's feelings, thoughts, or actions any more than I am responsible to *fix* them. Each person is responsible for healing him- or herself. By listening, I offer others the opportunity to express themselves and explore their own thoughts and feelings. My compassionate communication provides a caring space and honors both other people and myself in an honest and loving manner.

Your Own Spiritual Tutorial

- a) Whom do you "fail to communicate" with the most? (e.g., myself, child, boss, co-worker, parent)
  b) Why do you think it is a failure? (e.g., nothing is resolved, they don't understand my point of view)

- What repetitive pattern do you see when you converse with them? (e.g., always giving in, feeling frustrated, seeing each communication as an opportunity to win, seeing different viewpoints as wrong, jumping in to save people)

- How can you practice compassionate communication in future conversations? (e.g., listen without snap judgments, let go of a need to have a specific outcome, recognize that we cannot fix others)

Abundance—Yours to Receive

I FEARED ABUNDANCE. IT took a long time for me to recognize this limiting belief. I accepted that getting everything I wanted made me a greedy person because it took away from others getting what they wanted. It was evil to take more than a small share of the limited available resources. I can still hear that old message from childhood: "take only what you really need, and remember to leave enough for others." I heard it so often that I internalized this mammoth scarcity as a truth that led me to believe that it was selfish to ask for anything I wanted. If I did ask, I had to be prepared for disappointment because there was not enough to go around. Taken further, the belief meant that good things happened randomly and were frugally dispensed. I should take what was offered and be grateful for getting anything at all. With time and effort, I overcame this old programming and replaced it with my own truth. Spirit doesn't censor or limit what I can ask for and expect to receive. I am encouraged to go ahead and ask. There is an unlimited abundance for everyone, so go ahead and ask for love, hope, laughter, fun, health, peace, and abundant financial support. It's all good!

One word of caution: I learned that you cannot ask for something and then allow the old program of scarcity and fear to operate. This would be like purchasing new furniture and failing to be home to accept its delivery. I had to be present to receive my requested abundance. I know that because I am a divine human, unlimited abundance is my birthright. Spirit will never think of me as anything less than a perfect creator and will deliver what I desire. I know that it is time to listen to my divine, be clear on what I want, and stop believing the limited thinking of my human self.

Your Own Spiritual Tutorial

• How do you view abundance in your life?

• Are there areas where you block the generation or delivery of abundance in your life?

• How can you be more open to asking for and receiving abundance?

Let Your Divine Shine

LET YOUR DIVINE shine.
Playing it small serves no one at all.

Let your Divine shine.
Bring forth your light; trusting it is right.

Let your Divine shine.
Feel inner peace as you see the miracles increase.

Let your Divine shine, for it is time.

Your own spiritual tutorial:

- How do you let your divine shine?

Struggle from Conception to Death

Lᴉꜰᴇ ɪꜱ ᴀ struggle from conception to death. This statement creates a belief that whatever the struggle—physical ailments, emotional upset, demons, actions of other people—is our lot in this life and we must accept that fact. Repeated messages from family, society, and church similarly told us the greater the sacrifice, the more *good* spiritual points we earn. Spiritual points, also referred to as karma, ensure our successful passage into heaven on Judgment Day. I was shocked when I finally realized that I held this belief. I was not raised in a particularly religious family. Attending church was optional, and I was encouraged to question religious teachings. As my consciousness increased, I saw that this belief had been passed down to many in an almost genetic manner.

My awareness showed me that all struggles, large or small, are based on fear and resistance. At the root of most of my struggles was the fear of scarcity accompanied by my resistance to accept any abundance offered to me.

After significant reflection and meditation, I exposed judgments that perpetuated my struggle and threatened my overall well-being. My fear of rejection or loss of approval made me hypersensitive to others' opinions. My fear of scarcity and unworthiness to receive perpetuated financial struggles and encouraged me to reject opportunities to succeed. My fear of expressing myself honestly in relationships created feelings of resentment and anger. Struggle was not a requirement for living but a self-imposed prison that I created for myself through these limiting thoughts and beliefs. It was both sad and heartening to know that I was the jailer. It was sad because it was my own creation; it was heartening because I knew that anything I created could be changed and re-created.

Now when I sense that I might be struggling, I seek out the negative judgments that created fear of the situation. Once I am aware, I can replace the fear with the divine truth that I no longer need to create this struggle. I know that another's attitude and approval are not required for me to be happy and content. To this day, I quickly engage with Spirit and seek insight at the first sign of dis-ease to prevent myself from spinning it into a prolonged struggle. I am grateful for the wisdom to see that I create the struggle; therefore, I have the power to end it.

Your Own Spiritual Tutorial

- What are you struggling with the most right now in your life? (e.g., relationships, addictions, finances, career)

- What fears are perpetuating these struggles? (e.g., being alone, not being supported, not enough money, not enough time)

- How do these fears support your resistance to releasing these struggles? (e.g., I don't have to take responsibility for my feelings; I can't change twenty-four hours in a day)

- What new beliefs and actions can you replace the limiting one with to allow you to move away from these struggles? (e.g., I create my reality; I am worthy to receive abundance; I am intelligent; not judging myself and others harshly, taking night class to achieve my career goal)

Surrender—A Tricky Business

AFTER MONTHS OF meditation, classes, and effort to connect with my higher self, I felt so frustrated I finally called out, "Just give me a sign. Really, is that too much to ask for?" As I said this, a song came on the radio. I thought if I heard that song one more time, I'd scream. It was always playing! Then, I listened to the words: "I raise my hands and I surrender." Suddenly, it hit me, and I roared with laughter. I had asked for a sign, and it had been there all along. I simply hadn't been listening. In that moment, I knew why I did not hear the message. The concept of surrender was a thorny perception for me. My view of surrender meant giving up, giving in, or showing a sign of weakness. The song led me to examine my ego's definition of surrender, which was based on the concept of separateness and independence. If I surrendered, it meant that I "lost" a battle. Ironically, I had not realized until then that the battle was only with my ego, which projected the need to be "better," "smarter," or "more generous and giving" than someone else. The underlying theme was comparison and competition with others. Why was I competing and comparing? This is how the ego measures personal worthiness and craves other people's opinions. The ego lives only in the external world, a place where I would always find someone better, smarter, or more generous than me. The result is an endless roller coaster of feeling superior, followed by a crash of feeling inferior, as if I had to keep the secret that I wasn't really of value. My ego drove me to win at all costs, never give in, and never give up. This was no longer working, so it was time to listen to my soul's perception of surrender. Spirit's perception of surrender is an expression of courage and strength, not a weakness to be covered up. In fact, spiritual surrender requires the strength to overcome the ego's dominant but limited perspective. It requires the courage to adopt a higher point of view and release the need to compare and compete with others to build myself up. It is a simple and powerful view of my own worthiness being at one with Spirit and, indeed, all things. It was through surrender that I understood how I could lovingly serve others and myself.

Your Own Spiritual Tutorial

- How do you define surrender in your life? (e.g., admitting failure, giving up my own ideals and ideas)

- How does your definition of surrender affect your life? (e.g., It's stressful because I'm constantly seeking new ways to outperform others; It's depressing because I never measure up)

- What is a better definition of surrender in your life? How will this new definition affect your day-to-day actions? (e.g., Surrender is the strength to live my values regardless of others' opinions, and that will mean I feel more authentic; Surrender is the courage not to compete with others and to see my worth and the others' worth as equal)

Relinquishing Control

Bonds and constraints are linked to control.
They surround and tie me, refusing to let go.
Exhausted and running out of all hope,
Wondering how in the world I will cope.

How could I ever believe myself to be free
When only fear and illusion reside within me?
My ego is telling me that everything's fine,
Yet I feel a deep yearning I cannot define.

Slowly, I question the truth of my ego's big claims,
Knowing there is no one and nothing to blame.
This is my process, my own path to travel.
And gradually the illusions begin to unravel.

Illusions of struggle, conflict, and guilt
Seen now as the house that the ego has built.

The periods of doubt start to subside
As I accept my place along God's side.
My face now fully turned toward the light,
My heart knows the one truth that's right.

Being Divine is not an illusion,
It actually is the only conclusion.

Let Go...Let God

*L*ET GO AND *let God* are the two phrases that hold the key to joy, success, peace, and love in this earth realm. Intuitively, I knew this was my goal, yet I resisted letting go and trusting my inner guidance.

In this life, I defined myself by the roles I assumed, such as daughter, aunt, employee, and entrepreneur. In each role, I judged how well I managed the roles according to others' definitions of what constituted success or failure. Each role I assumed let me differentiate myself from others and demonstrate my value (or lack thereof) to my family, at work, and in my community and society. Each role required careful control and maintenance to measure up to others' expectations. Every role I adopted represented a greater occasion for fear of not measuring up. I invested a lot of time and energy trying to reinforce my self-worth as judged by others. I continued to subdivide myself into compartments—I had a work life, separate from my home life, separate from my social life. As my life became more fragmented, I was constantly in a race to hold it together. There was little peace or joy in keeping myself glued together. It was a tiring task and took time away from my opportunity just to *Be*. Yet letting go aroused an almost paralytic fear. What would happen if I let go? How would others value me? How would I value myself without their assessment?

In truth, letting go and letting God was my opportunity to surrender the ego's illusionary self and define my value from within. It was scary, but the alternative—namely, continuing to seek others' assessment of my worthiness—was no longer an option. I dug deep beyond the fear and discovered my true Self. My true Self doesn't need roles and judgments to feel worthy and valued. Over time, I let go of others' judgments and liberated myself to see my self-worth through my divine Self. I began to live with the strength and courage to be my authentic Self. My energy was redirected to my inner world of *Being* and consciously live whatever roles express my inner joy, love, peace, and contentment. Letting go and letting God meant I surrendered *my ego-based self* to bring forth *my true Self.*

Your Own Spiritual Tutorial

- What roles or masks do you currently assume in the world of form? (List all of them. The more you can identify, the greater your capacity to see which roles you want to release.)

- What judgments and expectations do you hold for yourself for each of these roles? (These judgments and expectations delineate how you are defining your value. Are these expectations realistic, or do they sabotage your ability to feel worthy?)

- What would happen if you released these roles and/or expectations? (For instance, what do you fear the most about letting go of others' opinions of you and your value?)

- What steps will you take to release those roles that drain your energy and how will you seek Spirit's support? (Baby steps are great. Remember you are the creator, and move at whatever pace feels safe for you.)

Harmony

HARMONY BLENDS OUR physical and spiritual beings into a single, joyful tune that is a balance of all the notes of life—highs and lows, vibratos and base. Living in congruence helps me intensify enjoyment of the simple pleasures of being in physical form, whether it's the kiss of the summer breeze on my face, the burst of flavour on my tongue when I bite into an orange, an intimate sharing of myself with a lover, the satisfaction of a deep belly laugh, or tears of joy and gratitude. Harmony is the perfect concert within me. Harmony replaces the striving or longing for what could be. In its place is an unpretentious contentment knowing all is as it should be. To live in harmony is to live in divine ease and trust my connection with Spirit.

Your Own Spiritual Tutorial

- How do you create harmony in your life?

- What seems to disrupt your spiritual concert—that is, what creates a sense of imbalance or out of sorts that you might not be able to put your finger on? (These are wonderful insights.)

- How can you create increased harmony in your life? (Remember we are all creators, and creation follows the process of thought, word, and deed yet not necessarily in that order. You can create harmony by changing an action, changing how to speak to yourself, or revising a limiting belief. It is your symphony.)

Playing Seek-and-Find

ONE OF MY favourite games as a child was hide-and-seek. In my eyes, it was a type of treasure hunt seeking my friends who were hidden. We took turns being treasure, trusting that we were worth the search and would eventually be found. I was a better seeker than hider because I liked being found.

As an adult, I have altered it a bit. Now it is more a game of seek-and-find. The principles are the same. We all have within us a variety of treasures waiting to be found. The riches include unconditional love, connection with our divine self, inner peace, and contentment. I know that our expression of Spirit is how we find these inner treasures.

When I know that I am cherished, I reveal that you are cherished. When I know that I am loved, I reveal that you are loved. In seek-and-find, I trust that all the treasures within me are also within you, for we are all one with the divine. Now for the next game…Tag, you're it!

Your Own Spiritual Tutorial

- What treasure do you seek from within? (We all have treasures to bring into this world of form. Don't be afraid to own them and share them with others.)

- What obstacles in your life keep you from finding your treasure? (In seek-and-find, you may need to expand your search to new areas beyond your comfort zone to find that rewarding treasure.)

- How can you overcome these obstacles? (Just as we are the creators of our obstacles, we also create our solutions.)

Growing My Garden of Dreams

My garden of dreams begins when I planted seeds of hope and desire. I tend my seeds with faith that my garden will succeed and bring forth my dreams. Dream gardening requires consciousness of my thoughts (the seeds planted) and their resulting outcomes (my creations).

It takes effort to plant and cultivate my dreams; however, I am free to shape them as I want them to be and create my unique crop. Like any garden, my "dreams" garden requires trust and faith. I'm responsible for nurturing it and removing weeds (negative thoughts) that I don't want. I recognize that Spirit is my co-gardener assisting with germinating the seeds, providing the sunlight, and allowing the miracle of growth. With experience, I have learned to trust my ability to select the best thoughts for me, trust my ability to nurture those thoughts into dreams, and trust Spirit to supply the magic needed to enable my dreams to blossom perfectly.

Your Own Spiritual Tutorial

- What dreams does your garden hold? (We are divine creators, and dreams are the foundation of what we want to bring forth in this life, e.g., having happy relationships, being a healer, writing a book, creating a charity to support a cause.)

- What thoughts have you planted to bring these dreams forth? (e.g., visualizing the garden in full bloom, acknowledging affirmations of success, holding yourself in high regard as you create your garden)

- What negative thoughts have you had to weed from your dream garden? (e.g., focussing on what you don't have, being impatient with yourself, blaming others for setbacks rather than learning from them)

Message from Within

―――――――――――――――――❦――――――――――――――――――

*L*ISTEN, *REALLY LISTEN.*
What do you hear?
The wind in the trees, birds calling to each other, and distant music carried on the wind.

Listen, really listen.
What do you hear?
Words floating through my head, creating stories and ongoing chatter.

Listen, really listen.
What do you hear?
Stillness grows, and I begin to hear my heartbeat defining the rhythm of me.

Listen, really listen.
What do you hear?
The whispers of my heart telling me the truth—the divine and I are one.

Listen, really listen to hear the message from within.

> *Your own spiritual tutorial:*
>
> - Take time to close your eyes, focus on your breath, and gradually quiet your mind. What is your soul whispering to you?

Guilt—Just Another Word for Judgment

―――――――――――――――∙❦∙☙∙――――――――――――――――

GUILT IS ONE of the many forms of self-imposed judgment. I feel a sense of guilt when I fail to live up to some criterion or expectation or, alternatively, find myself "indulging" in something I love to do. We refer to this latter experience as giving in to "guilty pleasures." These perceptions reinforce my own thoughts of unworthiness by making me feel undeserving or selfish. The continuous loop goes something like this: A good daughter should be looking after her parents, not off on some other continent having a good time. A good father would never have let his son become addicted to drugs. A good friend should keep her mouth shut rather than speak up because it might make the other person feel bad. I have so much while others have nothing, so I must give *everything* to them. Guilt lacks balance and keeps you from being able to enjoy things that make you feel good.

There are two underlying false beliefs that I thought were truths. First, I have "not measured up" to a belief of how things "should be." Second, by disappointing or angering others, I will lose their affection and love. It is a classic case of "shoulding'" on myself. The time has come to turn off the autopilot on the guilt trip. As a divine human, I am worthy to receive love, abundance, happiness, and joy without imposed conditions. The next time I find myself shoulding on myself, I will stop shoveling and bring awareness to my

Laura-Jane Cote

divine humanism. I will trust that I am worthy of accepting without guilt, enjoying without guilt, saying no without guilt, and just being without guilt. Furthermore, I know that just as this is true for me, it is true for all living in this time and space.

Your Own Spiritual Tutorial

- What judgments do you hold as false truths? (List all of them. The more you can identify, the greater your capacity to see how they are affecting what you tell yourself about accepting and loving yourself.)

- How are these judgments influencing how you value yourself and interact with others? (e.g., I judge that wanting to be rich is selfish and shallow; therefore, I sabotage myself from creating or accepting wealth)

- What would happen if you lived without guilt? What judgments would you need to let go of? (e.g., what do you fear the most about letting go of guilt of being wealthy, successful, or being able to do the things you love doing?)

- What message will you give yourself when you release your guilt? (e.g., You'd rather go with your friends for the weekend than attend the family event, so you change your message from "I must make my family happy—they must come first" to "I love myself as much as I love my family, and I am worthy of choosing what I love to do without guilt.")

Springing the Trap

From time to time, we all fall into the trap of putting fear first in our lives. The mind of our ego self does not trust the invisible, intuition, or Spirit. It knows only one response: fight, flight or freeze. The stress response is induced by fear. This response creates an unending circle from which the mind sees no escape. It is the heart that realizes the truth to end the ring of fear and springs the mind's trap. Let your heart guide you away from fear by responding from your divine self.

Focus on your breath—the breath that easily flows in and out, the breath that calms and restores perspective. As you let your heart assume the lead, you feel the fear dissolve and trust once again in the invisible, intuitive, and Spirit—your divine self.

While this sounds easy, it requires practice because our ego can be very persuasive. I experienced many moments of doubt and fear while studying mediumship to enhance my intuitive skills. My biggest fear was having to do trance channelling in class. My ego had a field day sending all kinds of messages: *Who do you think you are to be able to do this? Do you really think Spirit is going to talk through you? What if you get nothing? You will look like a fool in front of the class! It's just your imagination, anyway. None of this is real. I think I have to work late that day, so I can't go to class.* The fear was so great that a type of paralysis was setting in. I realized the futility of arguing with my ego's negative messages. Instead, I breathed—very, very deeply! As I focused on my breath, I felt a calmness. The doubt gradually faded into the background, and my resistance reduced. When my name was spoken and it was my turn, the fear briefly spiked again. I took another few deep breaths as I invited my guides to come forward to deliver their message. At that moment, I completely trusted that Spirit had my back and would speak through me. I opened my mouth, and a message came out. While I was aware that some words were forming, I had no consciousness of having formed these words or planning what was to be said. After the session, I knew—really knew—that Spirit will always be there and support me as I move past my own fear and learn to trust myself.

Your Own Spiritual Tutorial

- What fears does your mind perpetuate? (e.g., If I fail at something, I will look stupid; Speaking in front of people is impossible for me; I won't be able to utter one word; Telling my partner I want more in the relationship may make him leave me, and I can't survive alone)

- How do these ego messages support your resistance to releasing the fear and taking action? (e.g., Looking stupid will decrease my credibility at work, so I'd better play it safe; Everyone knows I don't like to speak in front of people, so they will find someone else to present my ideas; I am being unreasonable in my expectation of my partner in our relationship)

- What steps will you take to overcome the fear that is holding you back from being happy with yourself? (e.g., I know the fear will be there, but I will take the chance and do it; Mistakes may happen, but I will learn from them; I will present my own ideas and own them because no one ever died of embarrassment; It will get better; I will ask for help from Spirit to recognize the fear messages and replace them)

Golden Nugget of Me

As New Thought leader Christian D. Larson said, "Believe in yourself and all that you are. Know that there is something inside you that is greater than any obstacle."

Reflecting on this, I realize how many times I created "obstacles" in my life. No one can punish or keep me small like I can! How absurd it is to think that someone or something else created these obstacles. Obstacles are perceptions that I can overcome by using my inner strengths. I choose to dig for the inner strength of knowing that as a divine human anything and everything is possible. Recognizing this truth, I realize that inside me is a pure golden nugget of immense strength and value. That nugget is the real me, my divine self. I will have a wonderful day with my pail and shovel or backhoe (sometimes, I can bury things quite deeply) uncovering that priceless nugget of the divinely human me.

Your Own Spiritual Tutorial

- What obstacles (perceptions) do you create in your life? (e.g., I'm too fat to be seen in a bathing suit, so I won't go swimming; I can't write, so why bother journaling?; I've tried meditating but can't because my mind keeps spinning)

- How are these perceptions holding you back from living fully as a divine being? (e.g., seeing myself as inferior because of being fat, failing to have a safe avenue to express how I feel in a journal, giving up on practicing to connect with my inner self)

- How can you overcome these obstacles, and what perceptions can you change? (e.g., I won't let my size create fear about taking part in activities; I may not be great to start, but I will find the strength to continue; I can learn to express myself; My journal can be pictures instead of words, whatever feels good; I know I can connect to my inner self, so I will be patient with myself as I learn how)

- How will you celebrate overcoming these obstacles? (Be sure to celebrate frequently all successes, even the smallest ones. They all add up!)

Take Heart

THE WORD *HEART* has many meanings in this world of form.

Heart is the organ that pumps blood filled with oxygen and nutrients throughout the body and takes away carbon dioxide and waste to keep the body cells functioning.

Heart refers to a part of us that can be broken or shattered with sorrow or transport us to a place of joy and love.

Hearts can be "big," implying that the holder of this type of heart is generous and shares his or her good fortune with others.

Heart is a display of bravery in the face of adversity and challenges. It is the ability to overcome them when the odds seem stacked against the holder.

Heart is the seat of our Soul, the source of our true and eternal being, and it comes with a genuine spring of gratitude for everything.

When I hear "take heart," it signals me to go within and find my true essence—and with it, find my sense of love and hope. It is amazing how this single word describes every aspect of our being from physical form to spirit. Heart is universally expressed by hands held over the chest area where our heart beats. Regardless of the language I speak, the colour of my skin, or the circumstances of my life, everyone understands this simple gesture as an expression of love and compassion.

Your own spiritual tutorial:

- What does take heart mean for you?

A Final Word

Into your hands flows everything that you need and more. It is your responsibility to close your hands and accept that bounty with gratitude. This is a simple and profound truth. Many of us were raised with messages of scarcity and lack, of being unworthy, and that life is difficult except for the chosen few. It is time to unlearn these limiting messages and reclaim your truth that all you need and more is right here.

Throughout the process of co-creating this book, the *Real Me* emerged as I learned to consistently live authentically in this world. No longer do I fear that I am unworthy to receive the abundant blessings that Spirit provides. I trust that all I need do is ask and gratefully receive.

This is my wish for you as well as you embrace your divine humanism and find your power within to live authentically with joy, peace, and love.

Much love to you all.

About the Author

LAURA-JANE (L-J) COTÉ has been involved in health care for over 40 years. She began as nurse and moved into the healing arts.

She has studied healing modalities in Canada, the USA and England. L-J conducts workshops in Canada and the USA on Trusting Your Intuition, Psychic and Mediumship Development.

Her own spiritual journeys lead her to live in Hawaii for two years where this book was first conceived. Now residing in Victoria, British Columbia, she continues to have daily tutorials with her divine tutors and write.

Printed in the United States
By Bookmasters